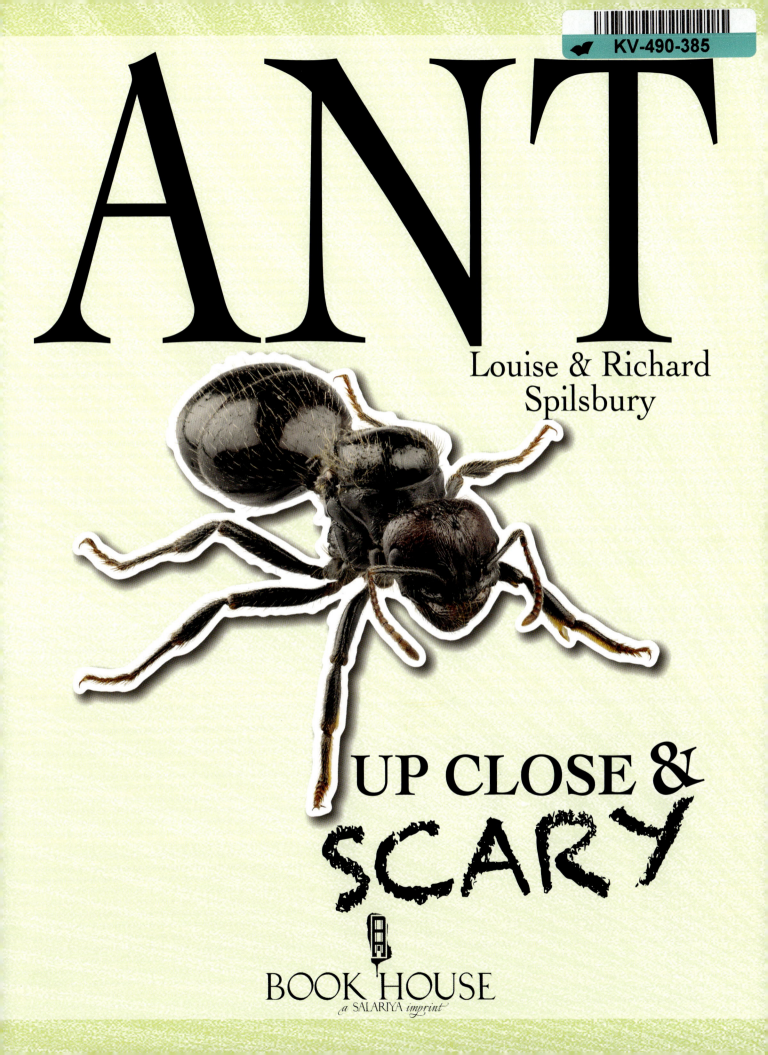

ANT

Louise & Richard
Spilsbury

UP CLOSE &
SCARY

BOOK HOUSE
a SALARIYA *imprint*

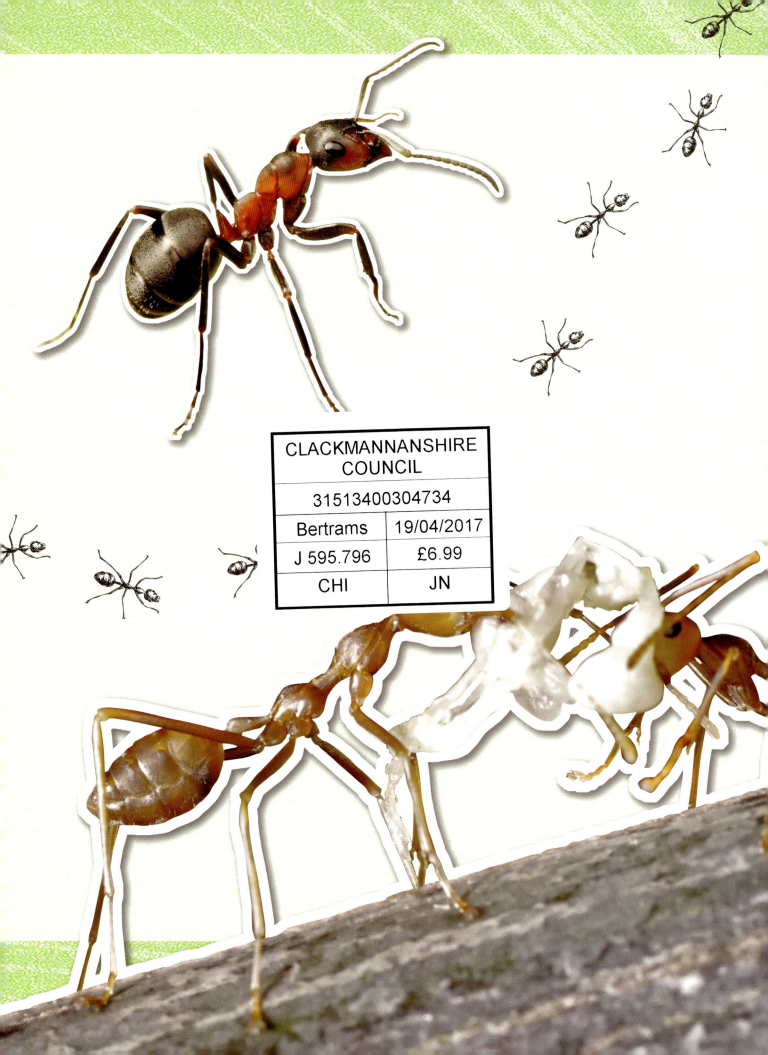

Contents

Ants

There are about 100 trillion ants living in every corner of our planet, except the freezing Arctic and Antarctic regions. These little insects are divided up into 13,000 different **species** or distinct types. Some ants are 5 cm (2 in) long, while others are so small that 32 ants in a row would measure only 2.5 cm (1 in) long. Ants can be black, brown, yellow, green or blue.

Up close, with their big jaws, ants look pretty scary, but the scariest thing about ants is that they always live in a group or **colony**. An ant colony can consist of millions of insects that attack anything in their path. There are colonies with only tens of insects, too. Not all ants in a colony look the same. Most are worker ants that do many different jobs for the colony, including collecting food. Soldier ants are the colony's army. They attack if the colony or nest is threatened. Queens are the most important ants in any colony. These females lay eggs that will hatch into new colony members.

This is a worker ant. In a colony, worker ants tend to the other ants, including the queen. They also build nests.

Soldier ant

Queen ant

Ants in a colony look different because they have different jobs to do for the survival and success of their group.

The body

Like other insects, an ant's body is made up of three parts, or sections. The head is used to work out what is around the ant. It has eyes, mouthparts and antennae (**jointed** parts for sensing). The head is joined to the **thorax**, to which the legs are attached. The thorax is attached by a narrow waist to the **abdomen**. This is where the ant digests its food.

Superpowers

Once a year, some of the colony's male and young female queen ants develop wings. On a warm afternoon, they swarm from their nest and take to the air. The flight is all about **reproduction**. Queens release a **chemical** to attract males, and **mate** with the fastest fliers. All the males die after mating, but each queen flies to a different place to start a new colony. Then, they bite off their wings because they no longer need them. If humans had this superpower, they would chew off their legs because they had reached their destination!

8

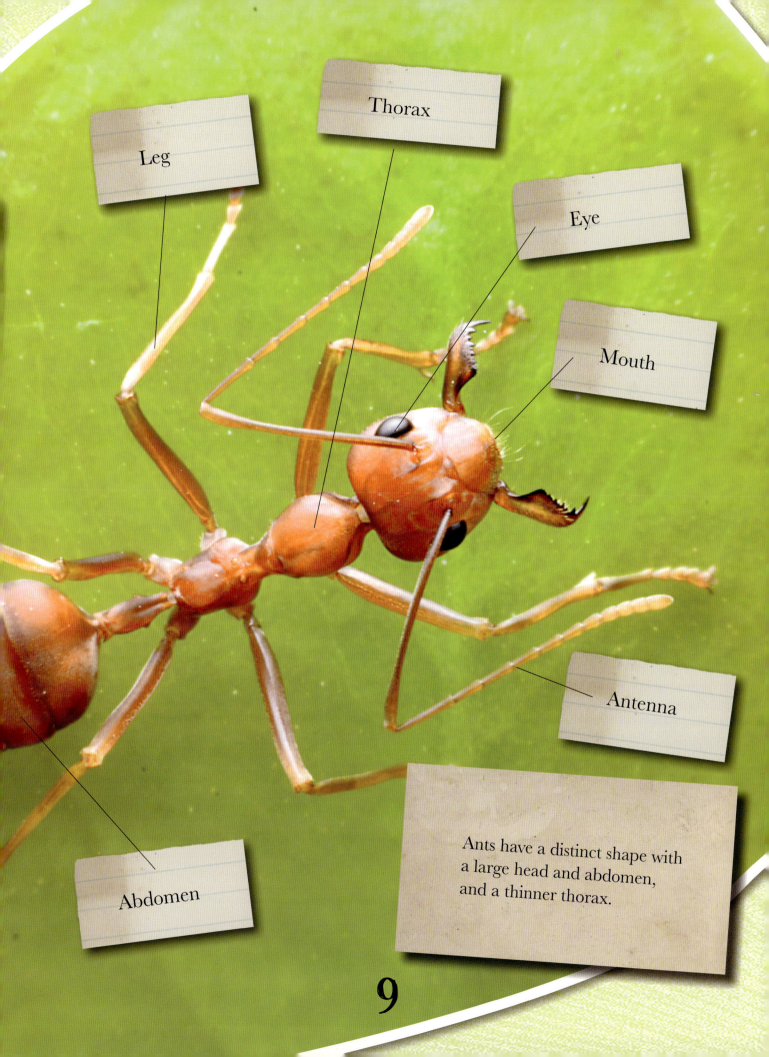

Leg

Thorax

Eye

Mouth

Antenna

Abdomen

Ants have a distinct shape with a large head and abdomen, and a thinner thorax.

The abdomen

An ant's abdomen is rounded in shape and covered in short bristles. Inside are many organs, which are important for a range of life processes. For example, tubes called tracheae move air to different parts of the body for respiration (breathing). Queens produce eggs in the abdomen for reproduction. The abdomen also contains two stomachs. One, called the crop, is for storing food for the colony. The other is smaller. It is for storing an ant's own food.

Superpowers

The honeypot ant can super-size! These ants live in deserts and other dry places where food is plentiful only in the wet season. In the wet season, special, large workers, called repletes, are fed so much sugary liquid by the other ants that their abdomens swell up to the size of cherries. In the dry season, other ants in the colony stroke the repletes to make them vomit some of their food store. If an average man's stomach swelled up that much, he would have a waist size of 5.4 metres (17.7 feet)!

10

Abdomen

Ants have **glands** in their abdomen that make chemical smells, which other ants recognise. They press their abdomen while they walk, to leave a scent trail that other ants can follow.

If ants look like they are kissing, they are feeding each other! One spits up food from its crop in the abdomen into the other's mouth.

Waist

Some ants tap their abdomen on the colony nest to warn ants inside of danger.

The head

An ant's brain is inside its head. The brain is about the size of a pinhead, which is quite big for an insect. Ants use their brain to process all the information from their antennae, eyes and other **sense organs**, to understand and remember things about the world around them. Ants see by using their two large **compound eyes**, which can detect movement but not very clear images. They also have tiny **simple eyes** on their head that can tell if it is light or dark.

Superpowers

Ants are clever for their size because their brains are so big. Their brain mass is one-seventh of their body mass. An average human weighs 62 kilograms (137 pounds). If humans had the same brain-mass to body-mass **ratio**, then an average brain weight would be nearly 9 kilograms (20 pounds). Imagine how big the person's head would need to be!

12

The ants with the clearest vision are bull ants. They can see objects up to 1 metre (3 feet) away.

Simple eye

Compound eye

Mouthpart

The antennae

Imagine having two bendy things sticking out of your forehead to smell with and to touch things. An ant's antennae are covered with tiny sense organs that can identify chemicals in the air. They can also feel air **currents**, **vibrations** and textures. A sense of smell is important for recognising other ants. If an ant has the same smell of the colony, the other ants welcome it. If the smell is different, then they may fight.

Superpowers

Fire ants dig narrow tunnels to make underground nests. They spend much of their lives moving through these tunnels, avoiding bumping into ants coming the other way. Sometimes tunnels collapse, but the ants never stumble because they use their antennae like grippers to grab on to the tunnel walls. If humans had this superpower, they would have stabilisers attached to their head. They would never fall over or bump into anything. Walking in a crowded place would never be the same again!

Joint

Antenna

Ant antennae have club-shaped tips and a distinctive elbow shape.

The joint and elbow shape of the antennae make them very mobile so the ant can feel all around its head.

Antennae can detect water in the air, helping the ants to find somewhere to drink.

15

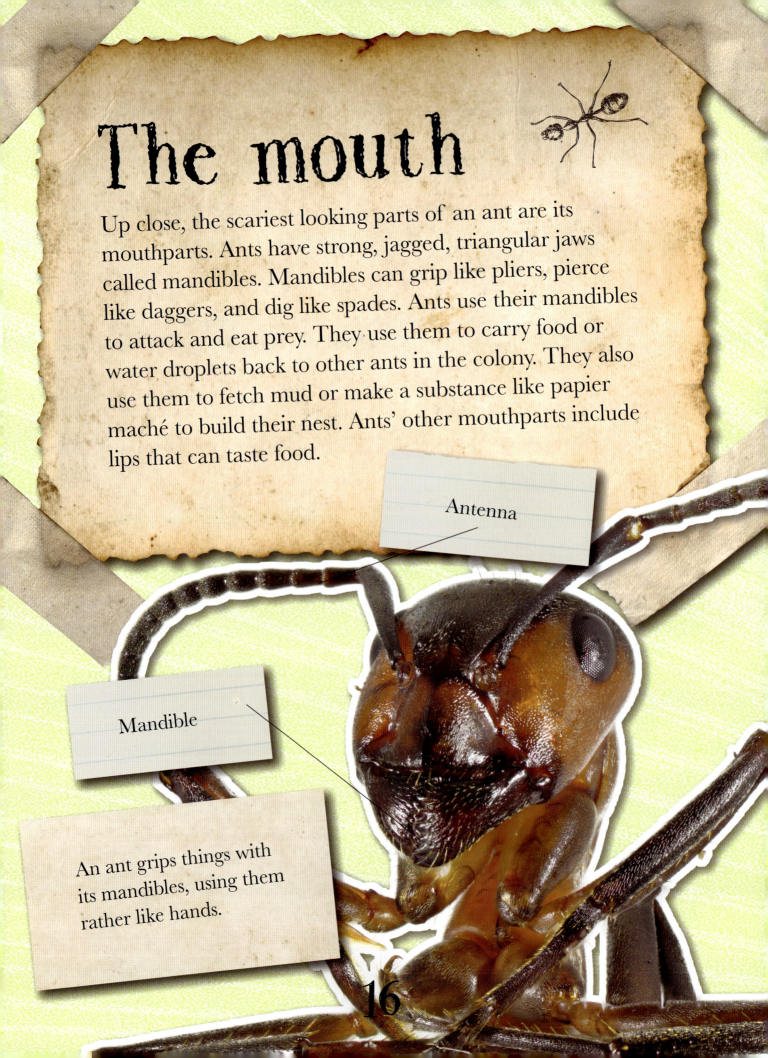

The mouth

Up close, the scariest looking parts of an ant are its mouthparts. Ants have strong, jagged, triangular jaws called mandibles. Mandibles can grip like pliers, pierce like daggers, and dig like spades. Ants use their mandibles to attack and eat prey. They use them to carry food or water droplets back to other ants in the colony. They also use them to fetch mud or make a substance like papier maché to build their nest. Ants' other mouthparts include lips that can taste food.

Antenna

Mandible

An ant grips things with its mandibles, using them rather like hands.

Eye

Lip

Ants sometimes carry other ants to a good source of food or a new nest site to help the colony.

Different ants have different shaped mandibles. For example, digging ants have wide ones to shift soil. Soldier ants have pointed mandibles to pierce their victims.

Superpowers

Trap-jaw ants have remarkable mandibles. They hunt with their mandibles wide open. The mandibles shut tight on prey if sensitive hairs inside are moved. The shutting speed is one of the fastest of any animal movements at up to 230 kilometres per hour (143 mph). That is 2,300 times faster than a human eye blinks! The mandibles are powered by large muscles inside the ants' head.

17

The legs

Ants are fast and **nimble** movers. Their six, jointed legs are tipped with tiny claws that give them great grip, even on smooth surfaces. Ants rarely lose balance because of the way their legs move. At any one time, three legs are in contact with the floor. As one lifts up, another touches the ground, so they are stable like a three-legged stool. An ant's front legs have special brushes of hairs on them that the ant uses to clean its **exoskeleton**.

Superpowers

Sahara desert ants live in one of the hottest places on Earth. They have extra-long legs that raise them above sand as hot as 60° Celsius (140°F), while they move around in search of dead insects to eat. These ants search up to 100 metres (328 feet) away but always return to their nests because they can remember exactly how many steps they have taken. This is like a person counting the steps on a 45-kilometre (28-mile) trip!

18

Leg

Joint

The end segment, or tarsus, has claws to help the ant to climb and to stop slipping.

Like other insects, ants have legs with five parts or segments connected by joints.

19

The stinger

An ant's **stinger** is the pointed bit at the end of its abdomen. On some types of ant, the stinger is the shape of a needle. This is used to inject **venom** under the skin of **prey** or any animal that is threatening the ant. In other ants, the stinger is nozzle shaped to shoot venom into the eyes or onto the skin of **predators**.

Superpowers

The most terrifying ants are jumper ants and bulldog ants. These insects can kill people. They are very aggressive and have no fear of humans. They bite with their long mandibles and then curl their abdomen to deliver a venomous sting. The venom is incredibly painful and makes the victim's flesh feel as though it is on fire. It can also cause death within 15 minutes, usually in people who are **allergic** to the venom.

20

The chemicals in ant venom, including **formic acid**, are made in glands inside the abdomen.

Some birds, such as thrushes, stretch their wings and stamp on ant nests so that the ants come out and spray formic acid on them. The acid does not damage the birds but it kills **mites** hiding amongst the birds' feathers.

Stinger

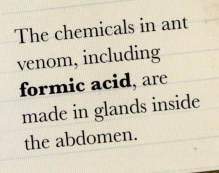

Abdomen

Ant venom can be 20 times more poisonous than a honeybee's.

Weaver ants

Ants make different types of nest including underground ones. However, the most remarkable is the nest of the weaver ant. Weaver ant workers make nests by bending leaves together. Some ants bite onto leaf edges and others link legs together with their claws. Many workers unite to pull the leaf edges together. Then, other workers carefully hold ant **larvae** in their jaws and tap them with their antennae. The larvae then produce silk to stick the leaves together.

Weaver ant workers have very strong jaws to grip leaves. They also use them to bite any animals trying to get near their nests.

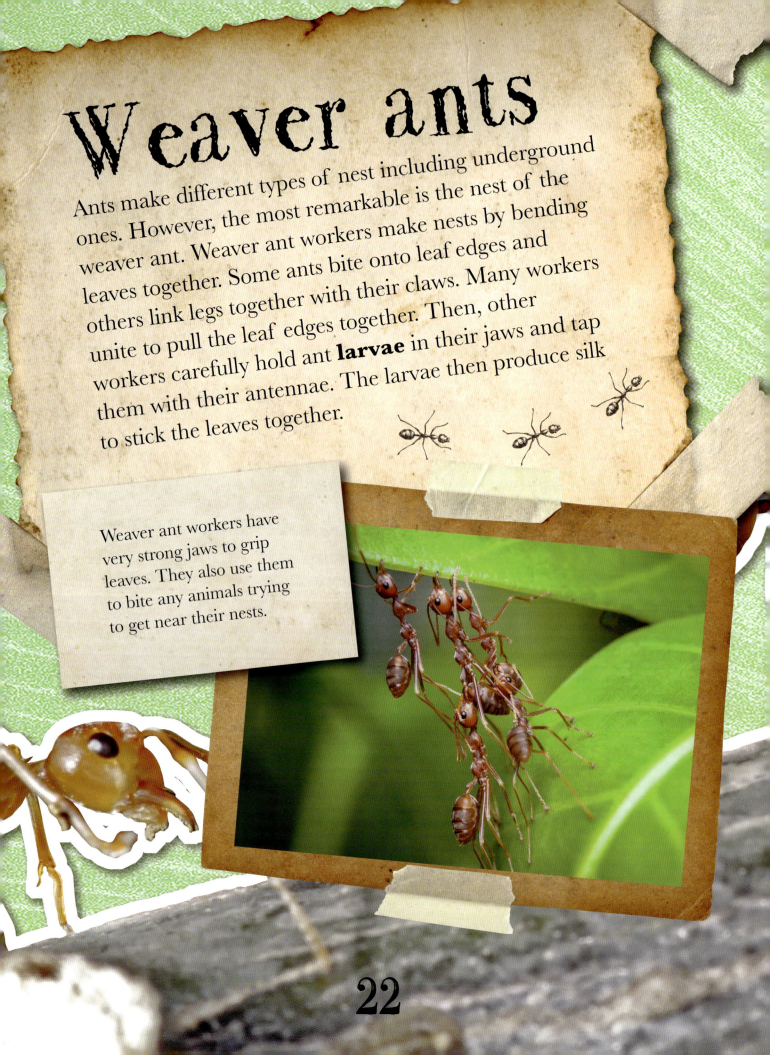

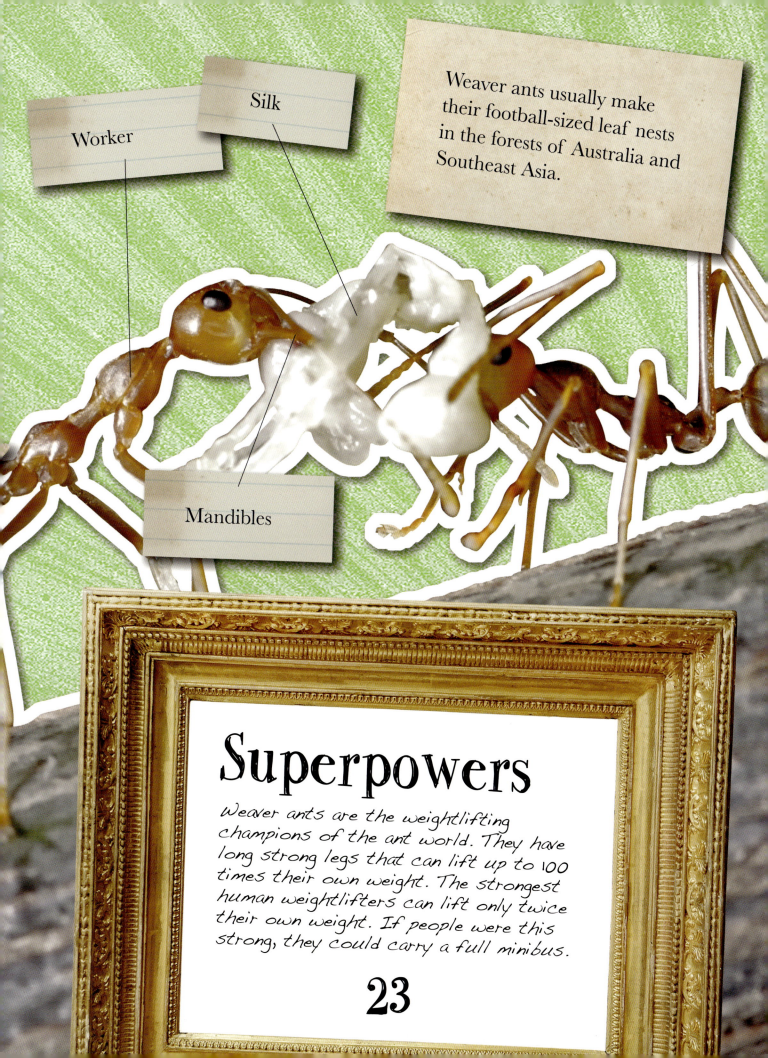

Worker

Silk

Weaver ants usually make their football-sized leaf nests in the forests of Australia and Southeast Asia.

Mandibles

Superpowers

Weaver ants are the weightlifting champions of the ant world. They have long strong legs that can lift up to 100 times their own weight. The strongest human weightlifters can lift only twice their own weight. If people were this strong, they could carry a full minibus.

23

Thorn ants

Animals climbing onto or trying to feed on some tropical acacia trees better watch out! Acacia trees have big thorns with a swollen base that may have a nasty surprise inside. Thorn ants live in the hollow insides and are ready to stream out to attack with their stingers. The ants defend the tree because the acacia's leaf stalks supply a sweet liquid, called nectar, which the ants like to eat.

Thorn

Ant

Leaf

24

Thorn ants defend acacia trees from all kinds of leaf nibblers, from giraffes to bugs.

Superpowers

Thorn ants are tree surgeons, too! Different types of thorn ant may compete for the same tree, so the ants that occupy one tree stop other types from getting onto it. They use their mandibles to trim off the buds at branch tips. This stops the tree growing outwards towards neighbouring trees so that other ants cannot climb across.

25

Driver ants

One of the scariest of all ant tales is about driver ants that kill people by swarming over them in death squads. This is not true, but driver ants are still a scary sight. They travel in columns measuring up to 100 metres (328 feet) long and more than 1 metre (3.2 feet) wide through African forests. A column may contain 20 million ants. They usually eat anything small in their path, from worms to insects, but occasionally, they have eaten bigger animals from snakes to horses.

Superpowers

Driver ants have fearsome mandibles. They are very strong with jagged edges that slice through the flesh of their victims. The jaws remain locked together, even if the head becomes detached from the body. Some people living in African forests utilise this when they get cut and are far from a hospital. They find driver ants, pinch the edge of the cut together and hold the ants to it. The ants' mandibles staple the wound together.

Soldiers form the edge of the column so they can defend the worker ants in the middle.

Worker driver ants in the column carry food, eggs and larvae.

Driver ant colonies live in one place for a few days and then move on in search of more food.

Driver ant columns may not be that fast at 0.014 kilometres per hour (0.009 miles per hour) – but that is not bad considering these ants average just 3mm (0.1 inch) long.

That's scary!

People are outnumbered by ants on the planet. For each human there are several thousand ants. In some places, there are enormous colonies of ants underground, stretching for hundreds of miles across. Powerful brains, strong mandibles, stingers and antennae are some of the body parts that have helped ants become so widespread. The way that jobs are split up between workers, soldiers and queens in colonies, and they way that ants communicate to coordinate these jobs, are reasons for their success.

In some places, ants are scary pests that can damage houses and sting people and pets. In general, ants are very useful. They kill pests on food crops and insects that can harm people. Ants help to eat up sick and dead animals, and food waste. When they dig into soil, they spread **organic matter** and air through it, making the soil **fertile** and helping plants to grow. Some ants **pollinate** flowers, helping plants to make seeds. So, the scariest thing about ants is how much our planet needs them to remain healthy.

Some ants are survival experts that escape floods by forming rafts and bridges! Changes in the Earth's weather patterns from **climate change** could still threaten ant populations.

Leaf-cutter ants bite off bits of leaves to take into their nest, where they turn it into compost to grow mushrooms for the colony to eat!

Glossary

Abdomen the part of an insect's body furthest from its head.

Allergic when something causes an unusual reaction in someone's body, such as a rash after eating berries or eggs.

Chemical a substance made by a chemical process.

Climate change the gradual increase in Earth's temperature, thought to be caused by human actions such as burning oil, gas and coal.

Colony a group of animals of the same type that live together in one place.

Compound eyes eyes made up of many lenses.

Currents movements of water or air in particular directions.

Exoskeleton the hard outer covering on the outside of some animals' bodies.

Fertile (soil) capable of growing many healthy crops.

Formic acid a type of smelly and burning chemical.

Glands body parts that produce special chemicals, such as venom or silk, with particular functions.

Jointed having two separately moving bones or body parts that meet, like at the knee joint on a human leg.

Larvae the wingless, often worm-like, form of insects when they first hatch from eggs.

Mate the way animals create new versions of themselves.

Mites small animals related to spiders.

Nimble able to move quickly and easily.

Organic matter part of soil formed from the remains of living things and their waste.

Pollinate when pollen from one flower moves to another flower of the same kind to make seeds and develop fruit.

Predators animals that catch other animals to eat.

Prey animal eaten by others.

Ratio the relationship that exists between the size, number or amount of two things.

Reproduction the way that living things create new versions of themselves.

Sense organs body parts that give an animal one or more of the five senses. The five senses are sight, hearing, smell, taste and touch.

Simple eyes eyes with only one lens.

Species a group of living things that are similar in many ways and can reproduce with each other.

Stinger the body part at the end of the abdomen that injects or sprays venom.

Thorax the body part between the head and abdomen with legs attached to it.

Venom poisonous fluid used to kill prey but also to warn off predators.

Vibrations movements up and down and to and fro.

Index

A

abdomen 8, 9, 10, 11, 20, 21

antennae 8, 12, 14–15, 22, 28

B

body 8–9, 10, 12, 26, 28

brain 12, 28

bull ants 13

bulldog ants 20

C

climate change 29

colonies 6, 7, 8, 10, 11, 14, 16, 17, 27, 28, 29

D

driver ants 26–27

E

eggs 6, 10, 27

eyes 8, 9, 12, 13, 17, 20

F

female ants 6, 8

fire ants 14

food 6, 8, 10, 11, 16, 17, 27, 28

formic acid 21

G

glands 11, 21

H

head 8, 9, 12–13, 14, 15, 17, 26

honeypot ants 10

J

jaws 6, 16, 22, 26

jumper ants 20

L

larvae 22, 27

leaf-cutter ants 29

legs 8, 18–19, 22, 23

M

mouths 8, 9, 11, 13, 16–17

N

nests 6, 8, 11, 14, 16, 17, 18, 21, 22, 23, 29

Q

queens 6, 7, 8, 10, 28

R

repletes 10

reproduction 8, 10

respiration 10

S

sense organs 12, 14

soldiers 6, 7, 17, 27, 28

stinger 20–21, 24, 28

T

thorax 8, 9

thorn ants 24–25

V

venom 20, 21

W

weaver ants 22–23

wings 8, 21

workers 6, 10, 22, 23, 27, 28